Facts About Countries
Pakistan

Ian Graham

FRANKLIN WATTS
LONDON•SYDNEY

Franklin Watts Australia
Level 17/207 Kent Street
Sydney NSW 2000

Facts About Countries is based on the Country
Files series published by Franklin Watts. It is
produced for Franklin Watts by Bender
Richardson White, PO Box 266, Uxbridge, UK.
Editors: Lionel Bender, Angela Royston
Designer and Page Make-up: Ben White
Picture Researcher: Cathy Stastny
Cover Make-up: Mike Pilley, Radius
Production: Kim Richardson

Graphics and Maps: Stefan Chabluk
Educational Advisor: Prue Goodwin, Institute of
Education, The University of Reading
Consultant: Dr Terry Jennings, a former
geography teacher and university lecturer. He is
now a full-time writer of children's geography
and science books.

A CIP catalogue record for this book is available
from the British Library.

ISBN 0-7496-6035-X
Dewey Classification 919.1

Printed in China

Picture Credits

Pages 1: Eye Ubiquitous/Jason Burke. 3: Eye
Ubiquitous/Peter Barker. 4: James Davis Travel
Photography. 7: James Davis Travel Photography.
8: Eye Ubiquitous/David Cumming. 9: Eye
Ubiquitous/Dean Bennett. 10: Eye Ubiquitous/Julia
Waterlow. 11: Eye Ubiquitous/Peter Barker. 13: James
Davis Travel Photography. 14: James Davis Travel
Photography. 15: Eye Ubiquitous/Jason Burke. 16: Eye
Ubiquitous/Jason Burke. 17: Eye Ubiquitous/David
Cumming. 19 top: Eye Ubiquitous/David Cumming.
19 bottom: Eye Ubiquitous/Jason Burke. 20: Eye
Ubiquitous/Jason Burke. 21: Eye Ubiquitous/David
Cumming. 22 top: Eye Ubiquitous/David Cumming.
22 bottom: Eye Ubiquitous/David Cumming. 24: Corbis
Images/Charles and Josette Lenars. 25: Corbis Images.
26: Corbis Images. 27: James Davis Travel
Photography. 28-29 Corbis Images/Jeffrey L.Rotman.
30: Eye Ubiquitous/Jason Burke. 31: Eye Ubiquitous/
Julia Waterlow. Cover Photo: Eye Ubiquitous.

The Author

Ian Graham is a full-time
writer and editor of non-
fiction books. He has written
more than 100 books for
children.

Note to parents and teachers

Every effort has been made by the Publishers to ensure
that the websites in this book are suitable for children,
that they are of the highest educational value, and
that they contain no inappropriate or offensive
material. However, because of the nature of the
Internet, it is impossible to guarantee that the contents
of these sites will not be altered. We strongly advise
that Internet access is supervised by a responsible adult.

Contents

Welcome to Pakistan

The Islamic Republic of Pakistan lies to the north-west of India. It became a separate, independent country in 1947.

Pakistan begins

At first, Pakistan was divided into two parts – East and West. In 1971, East Pakistan became the country Bangladesh. This left West Pakistan as the Pakistan we know today.

Below. **Vehicles wind their way through the Khyber Pass. The pass links Pakistan with Afghanistan.**

The Land

Animals

These are some of the animals that live in Pakistan:

Mammals:
Markhor (a goat, the national animal of Pakistan), wild sheep, wild goat, ibex, deer, antelope, bear, leopard, snow leopard, cheetah, lynx, grey wolf, golden jackal, striped hyena, wild boar, fox, macaque monkey, and porcupine.

Birds:
Golden eagle, black eagle, chough, black kite, sparrowhawk, falcon, kestrel, hobby, merlin, goshawk, partridge, rock nuthatch, crane and vulture.

Reptiles and Amphibians:
Crocodile, gecko, tortoise, python, cobra, horned viper, turtle, toad and various frogs.

Pakistan has high mountains, fertile plains and dry, dusty deserts. The Indus river flows from China through the length of the country to the sea.

High mountains

Three mountain ranges cover most of the land to the west of the Indus river. In the north, the towering Karakoram mountains include K2, the second highest mountain in the world after Mount Everest. In the centre lie the Sulaiman mountains. In the south are the Baluchistan highlands. Forces deep within the Earth are still pushing up the land, making the mountains even higher. This means that there are often earthquakes in Pakistan.

Below. **Average rainfall each month for Karachi.**

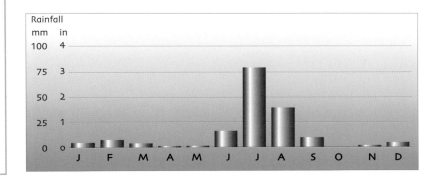

Climate

Pakistan has three different seasons. The cool season lasts from October to March. The hot season is from March to June. This is followed by the wet season, from June to October. During the wet season, plenty of rain falls on the flat land in the centre and east of the country. Rain pours off the mountains into the rivers.

The Thar Desert gets very little rain and it often has droughts. This desert is in the south-east and south of Pakistan. It stretches across the border with India.

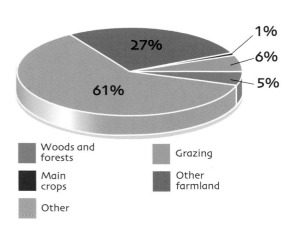

Woods and forests

Grazing

Main crops

Other farmland

Other

Above. **How land is used in Pakistan. More than half of the land is mountains and desert (labelled as 'other').**

Plants

Some of the trees that grow in Pakistan are: spruce, evergreen oak, pistachio, juniper, wild olive, ash, wild almond, fig, wild cherry and makhi.

Below. **The outer edges of the Karakoram mountains in northern Pakistan. The land has many small villages.**

The People

Five main groups of people, each with their own culture and traditions, live in Pakistan. They are the Punjabis, Sindhis, Pathans, Balochs and the Muhajirs.

Population

Pakistan's population is growing fast. It is now three times bigger than it was in 1947.

Below. **Like many Pakistanis, these fishermen have ancestors who came from India, China, east Asia and Arabia.**

Language

Pakistan's official language is Urdu, but less than a tenth of Pakistanis speak it as their first language. About half the people speak Punjabi. Government, the armed forces and universities also use English.

Purdah

Many Pakistani families follow a custom called 'purdah'. Women are hidden from view and they do not meet visitors. When they go out, women must wear clothes that cover their hair and whole body.

Changing culture

Many poor families do not observe purdah because their women have to work. In the cities, more and more women are choosing to work and not to wear traditional clothes.

Above. **Children wear the same traditional clothes as adults.**

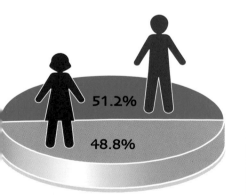

51.2%

48.8%

Above. **Pakistan has more men than women in its population.**

DATABASE

Ancient history

Stone Age people lived near modern Rawalpindi 50,000 years ago. By about 8500 BCE, people were farming crops in Baluchistan. Groups of people then began to settle along the Indus river. By about 2600 BCE, they had developed into the great Indus Valley civilization.

⊕ **Web Search** ▶▶

▶ http://www.statpak.gov.pk
Facts and figures about Pakistan, from the government.

▶ http://www.cia.gov/cia/ publications/factbook/ geos/pk.html
Information about Pakistan and its people.

▶ http://unstats.un.org/unsd/ demographic/
Facts and figures on the world's populations, from the United Nations.

Town and Country Life

Most people in Pakistan live in the countryside. Here, living conditions are very different from those in the cities.

City life

Pakistani families are very close. Many grandparents, parents and children all live in the same house. Homes and other buildings in the cities and towns are usually built of concrete or bricks. They have piped drinking water and sewers.

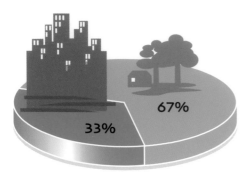

67%

33%

Percentage of people living in cities and towns

Percentage of people living in the countryside

Above. **Where people live.**

Right. **A farmer looks after his sheep in the Karakoram mountains.**

 The Islamic Calendar

Pakistan uses the Islamic calendar. It dates years from CE 622, the year that the prophet Muhammad (570–632) fled from Makkah (Mecca) to Medina, in Saudi Arabia. A year has 354 or 355 days, and each month is 29 or 30 days long.

Village life

Village houses are not as well-built as city houses. Often they have no piped drinking water or sewage systems. Villagers have to collect clean water from a shared well.

Home-grown food

Most families in the countryside produce some of their own food. Many families keep goats. They make cheese, butter and yoghurt from their milk. Bread and other food made from flour are eaten every day. Most families can afford to eat meat only on special occasions.

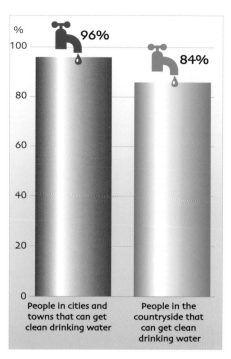

Above. **Percentage of people in cities and villages who have clean drinking water.**

Left. **A busy crossroads in the centre of Karachi.**

Web Search ▶▶

▶ http://unstats.un.org/unsd/ demographic/sconcerns/ densurb/default.htm Town and city population figures for many countries, including Pakistan.

Farming and Fishing

Farming and fishing

Weight in tonnes
Major crops:
Sugar-cane 55,200,000
Wheat   18,100,000
Rice   4,650,000
Cotton   1,768,000

Fish: 616,500

Farming is very important in Pakistan. About half of all workers are farmers. A quarter of Pakistan's total value of exports comes from farming.

Crops

More wheat is grown than any other crop. Most of the wheat is made into food and eaten in Pakistan. Sugar-cane, cotton and rice are grown, too. These are mostly exported. Some cotton is used in clothes factories in Pakistan.

Poppy flowers

Many of the world's opium poppies are grown in north Pakistan. Opium is used to make the illegal drug heroin. To stop farmers growing poppies, the government is giving farmers other seeds to grow instead.

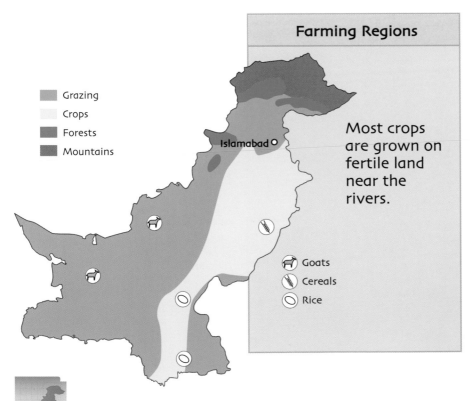

Farming Regions

Grazing
Crops
Forests
Mountains

Islamabad

Most crops are grown on fertile land near the rivers.

Goats
Cereals
Rice

12

Soil and livestock

Even in very dry areas, Pakistani farmers grow crops. They pump water from the rivers onto the land. But over time, as the soil dries, salts from the river water collect on the surface. This makes the soil infertile.

Livestock farming produces milk, beef, lamb, chicken, wool and leather.

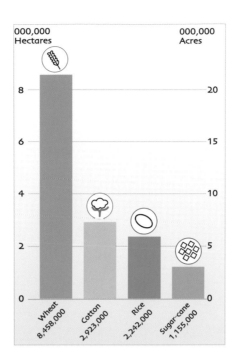

000,000 Hectares			000,000 Acres

Wheat 8,458,000 · Cotton 2,923,000 · Rice 2,242,000 · Sugar-cane 1,155,000

Above. **Main crops.**

Below. **A farmyard near Lahore. Most farmers use simple machinery, often pulled by oxen.**

Fishing

Most Pakistanis eat very little fish. On average, each person eats only 2 kg per year – about one-third the amount eaten in Britain. The fish caught include sardines, sharks, anchovies and shrimps.

Web Search ▶▶

▶ http://www.statpak.gov.pk/depts/aco/index.html
All about Pakistan's crops.

Resources and Industry

DATABASE

Amounts produced by mines and factories each year:

	tonnes
Cement	9,500,000
Coal	3,116,000
Iron	1,500,000
Steel	500,000
Gypsum	377,000
Soda ash	230,000
Caustic soda	220,000

Natural gas
  24 billion cubic metres

Crude petroleum
        20 million barrels
(1 barrel = 42 gallons/
        185 litres)

Most of Pakistan's natural resources are minerals. They are mined or drilled from the land.

Resources

Pakistan's minerals include iron ore, salt, manganese, sulphur and copper. Coal is mined, too, but it is mostly poor quality. Oil and natural gas provide fuel for power stations. Pakistan also has plenty of limestone, which is made into cement.

Below. **Some of Pakistan's trees are cut down and used as timber.**

Energy

Today, Pakistan uses three times more electricity than it did in 1980. More than half of the country's power stations burn oil, gas or coal to make electricity. Most of the rest is hydroelectricity.

14

Industry

Pakistan's most important industry is making cotton cloth. Companies that produce leather clothing, shoes and sporting equipment are growing fast.

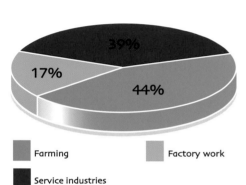

- 39%
- 17%
- 44%

Farming

Factory work

Service industries

Above. What workers do. 'Service industries' include banking, computing and insurance.

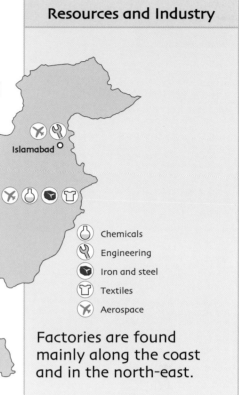

Resources and Industry

Islamabad

Chemicals

Engineering

Iron and steel

Textiles

Aerospace

Factories are found mainly along the coast and in the north-east.

Below. Young teenagers stitch together leather panels to make footballs.

Web Search ▶▶

▶ http://www.mpnr.gov.pk/
Pakistan Ministry of Petroleum and Natural Resources.

▶ http://minerals.usgs.gov/
minerals/pubs/country/
2002/afpkmyb02.pdf
Pakistan's mineral production.

▶ http://www.worldenergy.
org/wec-geis/edc/countries/
Pakistan.asp
Pakistan's energy production and use.

Transport

Mountain Passes

There are 200 passes through the mountains between Pakistan and Afghanistan. The most famous and important is the Khyber Pass (see the photo on page 4). It is 53 kilometres long and has been used by armies and camel trains for more than 2,000 years. Today it has a modern motorway and a railway line.

People can travel to and within Pakistan by road, rail or air. In towns and cities, people travel around on buses, taxis, auto-rickshaws and tongas (horse-drawn carriages).

Transport between cities

Modern, tarmacked motorways link the cities. The Karakoram Highway is one of the most famous roads in Asia. It runs from Islamabad to Kashgar in China. Rough roads and tracks link towns and villages.

Railways

Pakistan's national railway service carries 65 million passengers a year. It runs 228 fast trains, passsenger trains and mail trains every day.

Left. An intercity coach makes a stop on a road in northern Pakistan.

16

The chart on the left compares road and railway networks.

Kilometres | **Miles**

247,811 km
153,890 miles

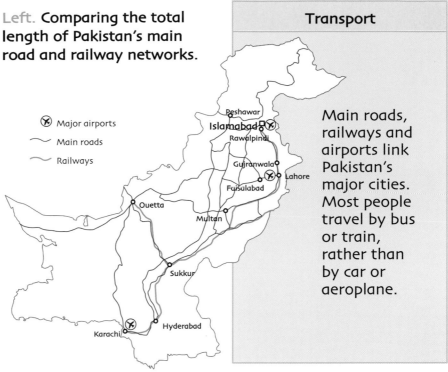

- 250,000 — 155,250
- 225,000 — 139,725
- 2000,000 — 124,200
- 175,000 — 108,675
- 150,000 — 93,150
- 125,000 — 77,625
- 100,000 — 62,100
- 75,000 — 46,575
- 50,000 — 31,050
- 25,000 — 15,525

8,163 km
5,069 miles

Railways | Main roads

Left. Comparing the total length of Pakistan's main road and railway networks.

Transport

⊗ Major airports
— Main roads
〜 Railways

Peshawar
Islamabad
Rawalpindi
Gujranwala
Lahore
Faisulabad
Quetta
Multan
Sukkur
Hyderabad
Karachi

Main roads, railways and airports link Pakistan's major cities. Most people travel by bus or train, rather than by car or aeroplane.

Left. In Lahore, most people use buses, auto-rickshaws or horse-drawn carriages to get around.

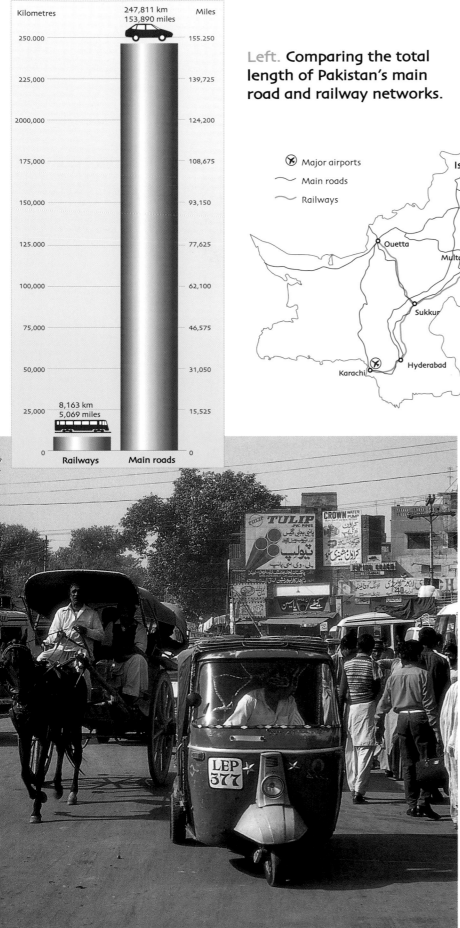

Web Search ▶▶

▶ http://pakrail.com
The railway service.

▶ http://www.piac.com.pk/
Information on tourist destinations in Pakistan.

▶ http://www.tourism.
gov.pk/guide.html
Pakistan's road, rail and air networks.

Education

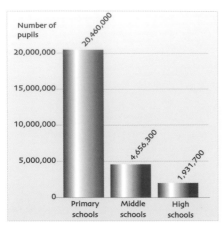

Above. **Primary schools are free. Most children do not study after primary school.**

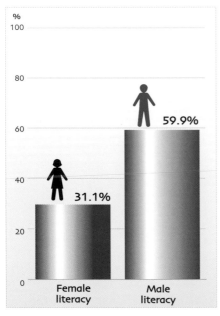

Above. **Numbers of men and women who can read and write.**

Pakistan has a well-developed education system. However, most families are so poor that their children have to work instead of going to school.

Schools

Children start primary school at the age of five. They go to middle school at the age of 10, and to secondary school at the age of 13. They study Urdu, English and Islamic studies, as well as other subjects. At the age of 15, they can go to a technical secondary school or to a higher secondary school for two more years. Some students then go on to university or college.

Literacy

Many Pakistanis cannot read or write. Literacy is lowest in the countryside and among women and girls. Less than a fifth of girls finishes primary school. Most state schools accept only boys, so some religious and political groups are setting up their own schools for village girls.

Below. A schoolboy practises writing Urdu using a slate and chalk.

Above. An outdoor class at a school in north Pakistan. All the pupils are boys.

Web Search ▶▶

▶ http://www.statpak.gov.pk/
depts/fbs/statistics/social_
statistics/social_statistics.
html
Facts and figures on
education.

▶ http://unstats.un.org/unsd/
demographic/social/
default.htm
Literacy figures for many
countries, including Pakistan.

▶ http://www.geocities.com/
Athens/Parthenon/8107/
univ.html
Universities in Pakistan.

Sport and Leisure

Pakistanis love sport. They do very well in hockey, cricket, boxing and squash. From small villages to cities, people play games and follow their favourite teams.

Hockey

Hockey is the national sport. The Pakistani hockey team has won several world championships and Olympic gold medals.

Below. **Polo is a sport that began in Pakistan and its neighbouring countries.**

Kabaddi

As well as cricket and hockey, *kabaddi* is also popular. It is played by two teams who each try to capture players from the other team. The game probably began about 4,000 years ago to train people in hand-to-hand fighting.

Right. **Children playing volleyball in north-east Pakistan.**

Cricket

Cricket is the most popular game all over the country. Players such as Imran Khan and Waseem Akram are world-famous.

Music

Until the 1980s, only traditional folk music was played on TV and radio. Traditional Islamic music called Qawwali is very popular. City people have begun to enjoy Western rock music, too. "Junoon" is the most famous music group. Its music is a mixture of traditional and rock music.

Web Search ▶▶

▶ http://www.sports.gov.pk
Pakistan's national and international sports teams.

▶ http://www.cricinfo.com
Cricket information and news, including details of Pakistan's team.

▶ http://www.junoon.com/home2.htm
History and music of Junoon.

Above. Muslim worshippers praying at a mosque.

The Hajj

Mecca is the birthplace of the prophet Muhammad, the founder of Islam. Every Muslim tries to visit the holy city of Mecca, in Saudi Arabia, at least once in their lifetime. The annual pilgrimage (religious journey) to Mecca is called the Hajj.

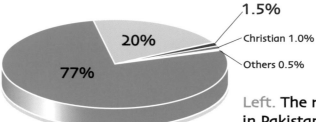

1.5%

Christian 1.0%

20%

77%

Others 0.5%

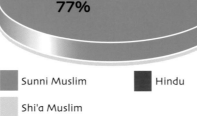

Sunni Muslim

Shi'a Muslim

Hindu

Left. The religions followed in Pakistan. Sunni and Shi'a are the two main branches of Islam.

Below. Most people shop for food in local street markets like this one in Quetta.

22

Daily Life and Religion

Everyday life in Pakistan is based on the traditions of Islam and the teachings of its holy book, the Koran.

Religion

Pakistan is an Islamic state but people can follow any religion. Prayer is central to the Muslim faith. People pray five times each day, usually at a mosque. A mosque is a Muslim house of prayer.

Marriage

Most marriages in Pakistan are arranged by parents. They introduce the bride and groom to each other. The bride's family give a dowry of money or gifts to the groom's family.

Food

Most Pakistani meals contain four main ingredients — bread, rice, vegetables and meat. The meat may be anything except pork, because Muslims are not allowed to eat pork. Spices are often added for flavour.

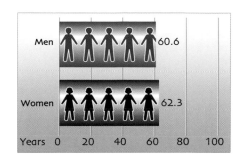

Above. **The age Pakastanis can expect to reach.**

Women's Dress

Most women wear the *shalwar-kameez*. The shalwar is a pair of loose, ankle-length trousers gathered at the waist. The kameez is a long top.

Web Search ▶▶

▶ http://www.tourism.gov.pk/events.asp
Information about festivals and religious events in Pakistan.

Arts and Media

The history of Pakistan and its art is shown in its museums and art galleries. Pakistan's cinemas, TV and magazines express the country's lively culture.

Museums

The National Museum of Pakistan displays pottery, metalwork, cloth and sculptures that are up to 7,000 years old. At Moenjo Daro, visitors can walk through the site of a city built around 4000 BCE. It may be the world's first planned city. In Karachi, the home of Pakistan's founder, Mohammed Ali Jinnah, is now a museum.

Below. **A cinema in Karachi.**

24

Cinema

This is the most popular form of entertainment. City cinemas show both foreign and Pakistani films. Cinemas in villages show only Pakistani films. Most of these are made in Lahore.

Television

Most of Pakistan's television channels are run by the state. More and more people can watch satellite TV, too.

Below. **Television and radio broadcast stations in Pakistan.**

Above. **This 16th-century painting in Lahore Museum shows men building a new palace and sculptors carving elephants.**

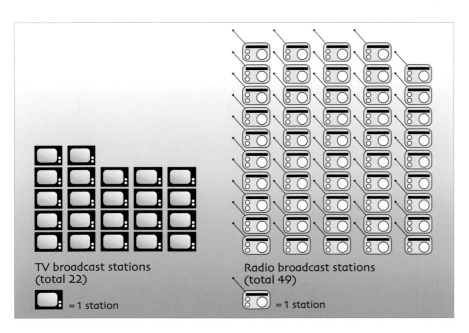

TV broadcast stations
(total 22)

= 1 station

Radio broadcast stations
(total 49)

= 1 station

🌐 **Web Search ▶▶**

▶ http://www.heritage.gov.pk/
Pakistan's traditions, culture and museums.

▶ http://www.ptv-news.com.pk/
Pakistan Television news.

Government

Pakistan has an elected president and two elected houses of parliament. The government, however, has often been taken over by the army.

Provinces

Pakistan is divided into four provinces and two territories. Each province has its own capital city. Islamabad, the capital of Pakistan, is in Islamabad Capital Territory.

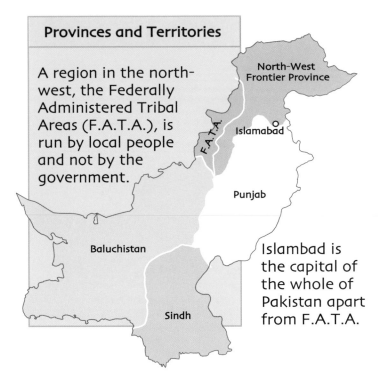

Provinces and Territories

A region in the north-west, the Federally Administered Tribal Areas (F.A.T.A.), is run by local people and not by the government.

North-West Frontier Province

F.A.T.A.

Islamabad

Punjab

Baluchistan

Sindh

Islambad is the capital of the whole of Pakistan apart from F.A.T.A.

Right. **The City Hall in Karachi, the capital of Sindh province.**

Parliament

The two houses of parliament are the National Assembly and the Senate. Each province has its own assembly, too. The president is elected as head of government for five years by parliament and the assemblies of the provinces.

Military control

In 1999, Pakistan's army took over the government and ran the country. In 2002, the military president, General Pervez Musharraf, began to give power back to parliament, and a new prime minister was elected by the National Assembly.

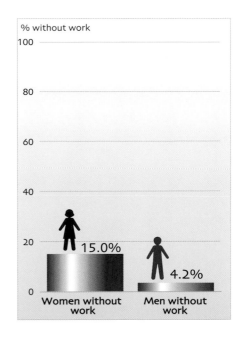

Above. **People without work.**

Left. **The royal palace at Hunz and the Karakoram mountains in Kashmir. Pakistan and India both claim Kashmir as their territory.**

Web Search ▶▶

▶ http://www.pakboi.gov.pk/
BFacts/provinces.html
Pakistan's provinces and their boundaries.

Place in the World

DATABASE

History to 1947

c8500 BCE Farming begins in Baluchistan

c4000 BCE The city of Moenjo Daro is planned and built

c2600 BCE Indus Valley civilization begins

1700 BCE The Indus Valley civilization suddenly disappears

518 BCE Persians take over Punjab and Sindh

195 BCE Greeks invade

CE 712 Arab Muslims conquer lower Punjab and Sindh

1163 Lahore becomes the capital of the Ghaznavid dynasty

1524 The Mughals enter Punjab and capture Lahore

1849 Britain takes control of Rawalpindi from its Sikh rulers

1947 British rule in India ends. Pakistan is created

Modern Pakistan is a recently formed country that is still developing its role in world affairs.

International organizations

Pakistan is a member of the United Nations, the World Health Organization and other international organizations. It also belongs to many Asian organizations.

Right. **Afghan refugees in a camp in Peshawar, Pakistan.**

Tackling problems

Pakistan is trying to increase the country's wealth by exporting more goods and stopping corruption. But the population is growing fast and many people are very poor. Since the US-led war in Afghanistan, many Afghans have fled to Pakistan.

Wars with India

Both Pakistan and India have nuclear weapons so their disputes over Kashmir could become very dangerous.

Below. **Pakistan's main exports and imports.**

EXPORTS
£5.93 billion (Cotton, sugar, rice, fruit, seafood, textiles, leather items, sports goods, carpets, handicrafts)

IMPORTS
£7.5 billion (Industrial equipment, vehicles, iron ore, petroleum, edible oil, wheat, tea, fertilizer)

Area:
803,950 sq km

Population:
144,616,640

Capital city:
Islamabad (201,000)

Other major cities:
Karachi (12,100,000)
Lahore (6,350,000)
Faisalabad (1,920,000)
Rawalpindi (920,000)
Hyderabad (795,000)

Longest rivers:
Indus (3180 km of which
2,896 km is in Pakistan)
Sutlej (1,551 km)
Chenab (1,242 km)
Ravi (901 km)
Jhelum (825 km)

Highest mountain:
K2, also known as Mount
Godwin Austen (8,611 m)

Longest glaciers:
Siachin (75 km)
Baltoro (62 km)
Batura (55 km)

Currency:
Pakistani rupee

Flag:
Green with a white crescent
and star in the centre, and a
vertical white band on the
left side

Languages:
Official language: Urdu.
English and Punjabi are
widely spoken. Sindhi,
Siraiki, Pashtu, Baluchi,
Hindko, Brahui and
Burushaski are also spoken

Major resources:
Natural gas, oil, coal, iron
ore, copper, salt, limestone

Major exports:
Clothes, rice, cotton, leather
goods, sports shoes

**National holidays and
major events:**
March 23: Pakistan Day
May 1: International
    Labour Day
August 14: Independence
    Day
September 6: Defence of
    Pakistan Day
September 11: Anniversary
    of the death of Quaid-e-
    Azam (founder of
    Pakistan)
Religious holidays are
based on the lunar
calendar and so fall on
different dates each year

Religions:
Mainly Muslim, also Hindu
and Christian

Key Words

ANCESTORS
People, such as grandparents, from whom you are descended.

ARABIA
Part of Asia including modern Syria, Iraq, Lebanon, Saudi Arabia, Oman and neighbouring countries.

ARMED FORCES
The army, navy and air forces; also known as the military or military forces.

AUTO-RICKSHAW
A small passenger vehicle powered by a motor scooter.

CLIMATE
The usual weather at different times of the year.

CORRUPTION
Using a position of power for your own gain, such as taking bribes.

CROPS
Plants grown for food or for products to sell, such as cotton.

CULTURE
The beliefs and customs of a group of people.

DOWRY
Money or goods given by a woman or her family to the man she is going to marry.

DROUGHT
A long period with no rain.

ELECTED
Chosen by voting.

EXPORTS
Goods or services sold to other countries.

FERTILE
Good for growing crops.

GOVERNMENT
The group of people who manage a country.

HYDROELECTRICITY
Electricity made from the power of running water.

IMPORTS
Goods bought from abroad.

NUCLEAR WEAPONS
Bombs, missiles or explosives produced by splitting atoms of the metal uranium to release energy.

LITERACY
The ability to read and write.

OFFICIAL LANGUAGE
Language usually used by people working in schools, government and law courts.

PASS
Natural gap between high mountains.

POPULATION
All the people who live in a particular area.

PROVINCE
Part of a country, often with its own local government.

RESOURCES
Materials that can be used to make goods or electricity, such as iron and coal.

Index